Easy-Step Books

Painting

Contents

Introduction

Painting is one of the simplest do-it-yourself tasks. It requires only a minimal investment in tools, and paint is readily available in a seemingly endless array of colors and sheens. Yet few projects can so profoundly change the look and appeal of a home. So it is worthwhile to make the effort to learn how to produce professional results.

Paint can decorate and protect all kinds of surfaces. Selecting the right color requires some understanding of how combinations of colors work together. You should learn how colors can "warm" or "cool" a room and how different colors can alter our moods. For proper protection, surfaces must be prepared thoroughly and coated with the right combination of primer and paint.

Painting is a one-stop guide to planning and applying paint to interior and exterior surfaces. It covers all phases of the painting project and includes tips on how to produce some decorative finishes. A troubleshooting section helps you diagnose and correct problem areas. For best results, read through the entire book before you begin any work. Your task will be easier and more satisfactory if you make the effort now to understand the whole process, step-by-step.

Switch-plate cover removed

Patched areas

Furniture covered with plastic

Floor protected

Selecting a Paint

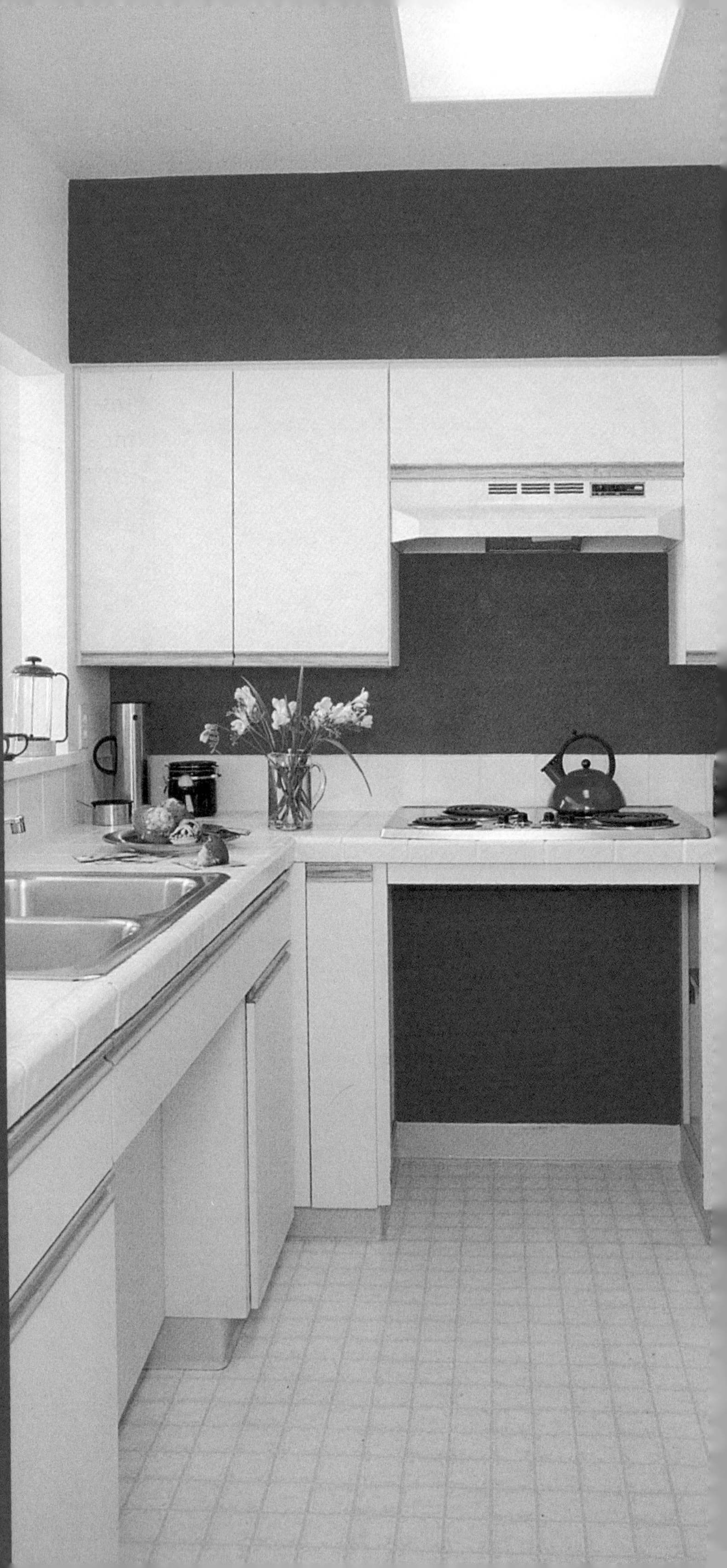

Assess color needs

Choose colors that please you personally and
coordinate with the rest of the house. But consider
that color is more than just an aesthetic element;
it also possesses qualities that can affect us physio-
logically and emotionally. Rooms painted in "warm" colors
(such as yellow or red) seem warmer than rooms painted
white or a cool blue. A red room can actually increase your
heart rate, whereas the same room painted green can induce
a restful and calming mood. Pale shades impart openness,
whereas dark colors feel cozier.

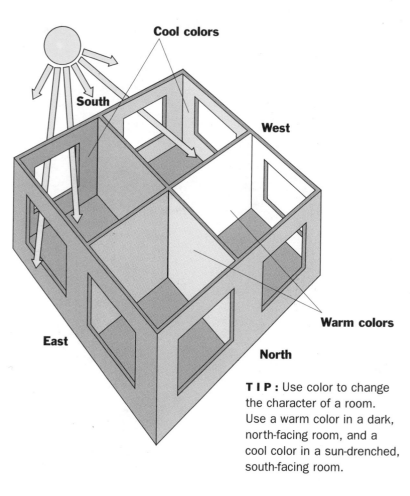

Cool colors

South

West

Warm colors

East

North

T I P : Use color to change
the character of a room.
Use a warm color in a dark,
north-facing room, and a
cool color in a sun-drenched,
south-facing room.

Choose color schemes

Colors rarely exist on their own. They rely on other colors to help define and enhance them. A paint dealer can help you understand the principles of the color wheel and the combinations of colors that best complement each other. Look for inspiration in nature, browse through furniture showrooms, and peruse home-decorating magazines. If you will be using something other than neutral fabrics, be sure to select the fabrics before buying paint. Paint color can always be adjusted; fabrics can't.

Pink

White   Yellow

White

Sandy or pinkish

Blue

Gray

Wood—clear finish

Reddish brick-colored tiles

Select a sheen

Sheen refers to the amount of light reflected by a paint. It affects both appearance and performance. Nonreflective flat (matte) paints are good for living room walls and ceilings, dining rooms, and master bedrooms. Eggshell (satin) paints have a soft luster. They are suitable for walls in children's rooms, hallways, stairways, family rooms, and bathrooms. Semigloss (enamel) paints are excellent for walls subject to heavy wear and frequent cleaning. Gloss paints have a hard, shiny surface and are a good choice for kitchen and bathroom walls.

Choosing Sheen

Interiors

Area	Best Choice	Acceptable Choice
Bedroom, Ceilings, Dining room, Living room	Flat	Eggshell
Bath, Hallway, Kids' room, Kitchen, Playroom	Eggshell (Satin)	Semigloss
Doors, Trim, Windows	Semigloss or gloss	Eggshell

Exteriors

Area	Best Choice	Acceptable Choice
Walls	Eggshell	Semigloss
Deck, Porch, Stairs	Porch and floor enamel	
Doors, Windows	Semigloss	Gloss or high gloss

TIP: Enamel paint offers the best stain and abrasion resistance. Its easy-to-clean surface makes it ideal for kitchens, bathrooms, door trim, and other high-maintenance areas.

4 Latex or alkyd

Latex paints contain vinyl or acrylic resins in a water-thinned medium. Higher-quality latex paints have the highest percentage of acrylic resins. Latex paints dry quickly and clean up with soap and water. They are a popular and durable choice for interiors and exteriors. Alkyd paints have largely replaced oil-based paints, even though the latter term is still used. Their synthetic resins are solvent-thinned, which means they must be cleaned with solvents (turpentine or mineral spirits). They also dry more slowly.

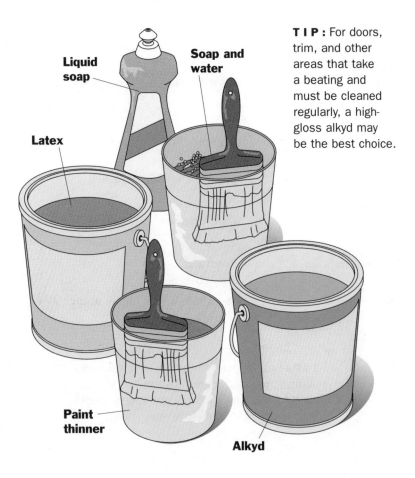

Liquid soap

Soap and water

Latex

Paint thinner

Alkyd

T I P : For doors, trim, and other areas that take a beating and must be cleaned regularly, a high-gloss alkyd may be the best choice.

Estimate quantity

5

Calculate the perimeter of the room to be painted (length doubled plus width doubled). Multiply the perimeter by the wall height to find the total square footage of the wall area. Subtract 21 square feet for each standard door and 15 square feet for each standard window. Buy 1 gallon for each 300 square feet, even if the can promises to cover more. Custom-mixed colors can vary by batch, so have more than enough mixed at the same time. You will want to have some extra on hand for touch-ups.

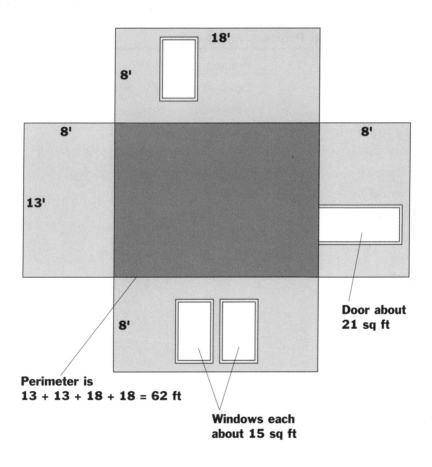

18'

8'

8'

8'

13'

Door about 21 sq ft

Perimeter is 13 + 13 + 18 + 18 = 62 ft

8'

Windows each about 15 sq ft

Choose a primer or sealer

When painting over exposed wood, wallboard, or plaster, first apply a primer (often called a primer/sealer). The primer will seal the uncoated surface and provide "tooth" for the paint. Primers are available in latex (water-based) and alkyd (oil-based) formulations. Some manufacturers offer primers intended specifically for unpainted wallboard. When painting over a "bleeding" wood, such as redwood or cedar, use a primer/sealer formulated to prevent extractive bleeding. You can paint over either type with latex or alkyd paint.

Where to Use Primers and Sealers

Surface	Product
New wallboard	Latex primer or wallboard PVA sealer
New plaster	Latex or alkyd primer
Painted wallboard, plaster	Alkyd or latex primer
Bare wood	Shellac; alkyd stain-killing primer/sealer
Painted wood	Spot-prime repairs with pigmented shellac
Masonry	Alkyd or latex exterior sealer
Metal	Metal primer

7 Choose premium paint

Most manufacturers make several grades of paint, sold at different prices. It is almost always worthwhile to buy the best paint you can afford.

A high-quality paint will have better pigment, more and better binders (usually resins), and often will contain titanium dioxide—an exceptionally opaque white pigment. A gallon of premium paint may cost two or three times more than a low-cost grade, but it will spread easier, splatter less, level better, and last much longer, making it less expensive in the long run.

T I P : Because it contains more pigment, a high-quality paint will hide better than an inferior grade. You'll be able to use less or apply fewer coats.

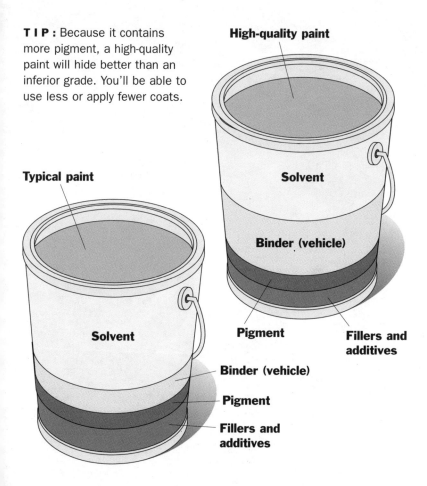

High-quality paint

Typical paint

Solvent

Binder (vehicle)

Pigment

Fillers and additives

Solvent

Binder (vehicle)

Pigment

Fillers and additives

Brushes

Paint applied properly with a high-quality brush will provide the best coverage and finish with the least mess. Most work can be handled by the three brushes shown below. Natural-bristle brushes are used only with alkyd or oil-based paints. Synthetic-filament brushes can be used with all kinds of paint. Brushes that combine nylon and polyester filaments are a good all-purpose choice. Better-quality brushes are usually the best investment. Look for long, dense bristles or filaments with chisel (tapered) tips.

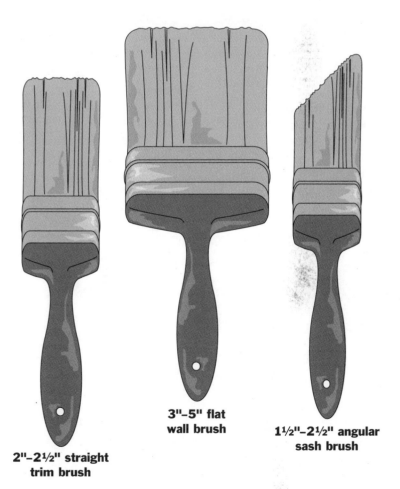

3"–5" flat wall brush

1½"–2½" angular sash brush

2"–2½" straight trim brush

2 Rollers and pads

Rollers excel at covering walls and ceilings quickly, whereas sponge pads handle corners with ease. A roller should have a sturdy steel frame, nylon bearings, a 9-inch wire sleeve, and enclosed ends. The handle should be threaded to hold an extension pole. Choose roller covers to match the type of paint and texture of the surface to be covered. Pads apply paint faster than brushes and, often, smoother than rollers. They are good for edging, can be used with alkyd or latex paints, and are disposable.

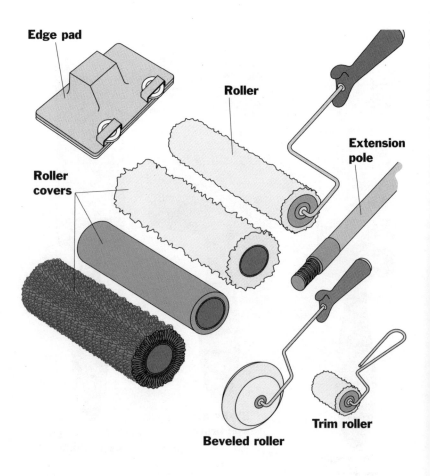

Edge pad

Roller

Extension pole

Roller covers

Beveled roller

Trim roller

Sprayers

Nothing applies paint faster than a sprayer. When used properly, a sprayer can produce an almost flawless finish. But sprayers require much more setup and cleanup time than brushes and rollers. Conventional handheld sprayers require a compressor and are best for oil-based finishes on trim, doors, and cabinets. Airless sprayers are popular with professionals for applying latex paint to walls and other large surfaces. Both types waste a lot of paint. Modern high-volume, low-pressure (HVLP) sprayers are much more efficient, but may apply paint unevenly.

Handheld sprayer

Airless sprayer

HVLP sprayer

T I P : Rent professional-quality spray equipment from paint suppliers and rental companies. Affordable handheld sprayers are useful for painting complex surfaces such as latticework and shutters.

4 Ladders and scaffolding

Two sturdy 6-foot stepladders and a 12-foot-long 2×10 are adequate for most interior and many exterior paint jobs. Create a makeshift scaffold by resting the plank on the ladder steps (with the steps facing each other), extending it 1 foot beyond the back legs. Secure the plank with clamps. Outdoors you will need an extension ladder capable of safely reaching the highest parts of the house. A multisegment ladder can be adjusted to serve as a stepladder, extension ladder, and scaffolding platform.

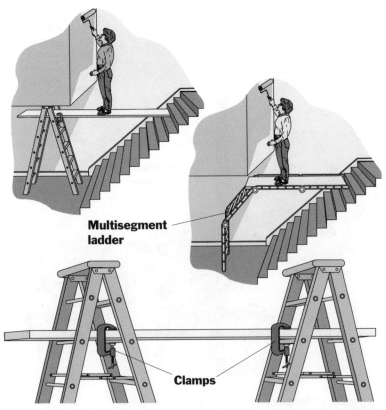

Multisegment ladder

Clamps

TIP: Consider renting scaffolding if you have a lot of prep and painting to do on upper stories.

5 Other tools

To remove old paint, you will need a paint scraper, wire brushes, sandpaper, and perhaps a power sander and heat gun. For protecting surfaces from unwanted paint, drop cloths and masking tape are indispensable. Plastic sheeting is inexpensive and suitable for small jobs, but canvas drop cloths are rugged, easy to walk on, and will absorb paint drips. For personal safety you will want safety glasses or goggles, dust masks, and gloves. Clean and dispose of all materials according to manufacturer's instructions.

Heat gun Goggles Scraper Wire brush Dust mask Respirator Putty knives Sanding block Masking tape Painter's tape

Preparing to Paint

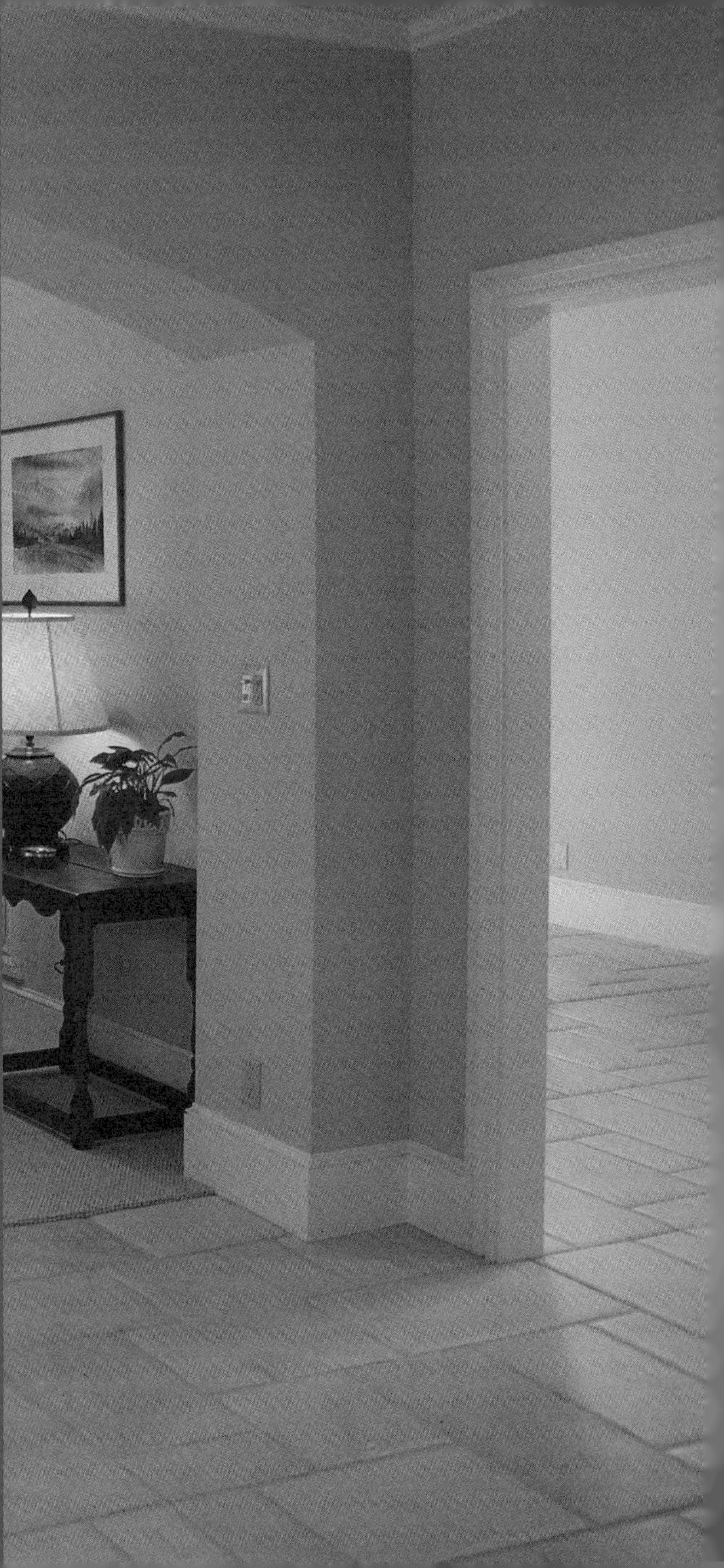

1 Remove old paint

Strip paint or varnish from smooth woodwork and paneling by dry scraping, followed by light sanding. If the paint is damaged or layered thickly, or the surface is irregularly shaped, use a chemical paint stripper (read and follow instructions carefully). Remove loose paint on exterior walls with a scraper, then finish the job with a power sander. A heat gun can be effective for removing oil-based paint, but should be used only with extreme caution. Heat softens the paint, which is removed with a scraper or putty knife.

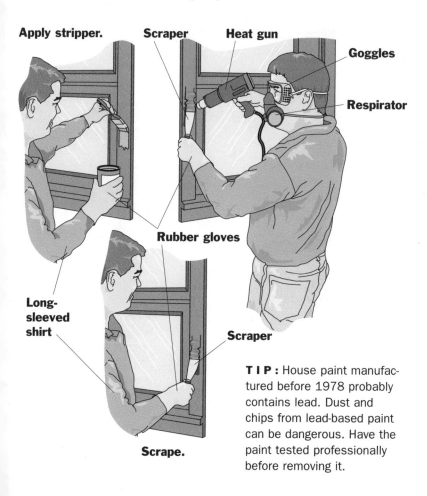

Apply stripper.

Scraper   Heat gun

Goggles

Respirator

Rubber gloves

Long-sleeved shirt

Scraper

Scrape.

T I P : House paint manufactured before 1978 probably contains lead. Dust and chips from lead-based paint can be dangerous. Have the paint tested professionally before removing it.

21

2 Patch cracks and holes

Fill small holes with spackling compound applied with a 2-inch putty knife. If the edges are rough or broken, cover with a self-sticking repair patch or fiberglass-mesh tape. Cover with spackling or joint compound. Sand when dry. For larger holes in wallboard, cut a wallboard patch to cover the damaged area, trace around it on the wall, and cut along the outline. If there are no exposed studs for attaching the patch, cut and install backing, as shown. Apply wallboard tape and joint compound.

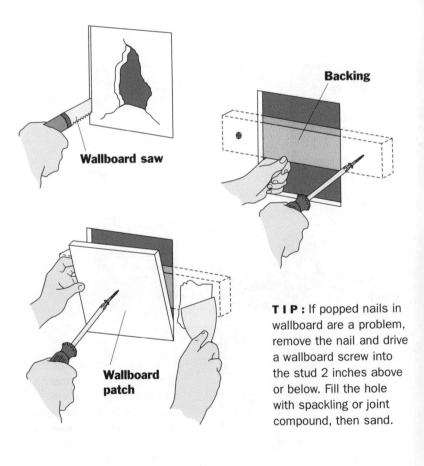

Backing

Wallboard saw

Wallboard patch

T I P : If popped nails in wallboard are a problem, remove the nail and drive a wallboard screw into the stud 2 inches above or below. Fill the hole with spackling or joint compound, then sand.

Fill small holes and cracks in plaster with spackling or joint compound. Remove loose plaster first. Moderately sized holes can be covered with plastic patching tape or with self-sticking fiberglass-mesh tape covered by one or two layers of joint compound. Repair large holes by scraping away loose plaster. Apply a latex bonding agent as directed. Mix a small batch of patching plaster, then apply with a 6-inch knife. Work the plaster into the corners. For holes larger than ¼-inch deep, apply a second layer. Sand as needed.

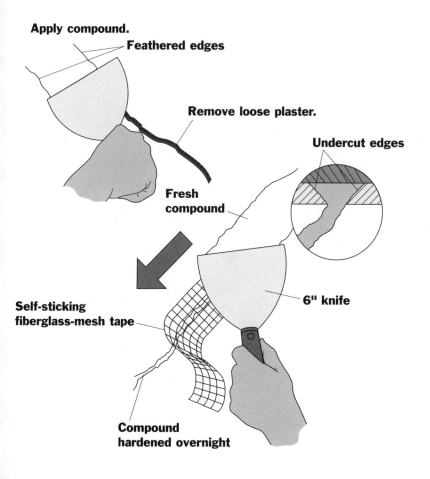

Apply compound.

Feathered edges

Remove loose plaster.

Undercut edges

Fresh compound

Self-sticking fiberglass-mesh tape

6" knife

Compound hardened overnight

Drape and mask

To drape walls, press the top half of 1½- or 2-inch masking tape along the top of the wall. Push plastic sheeting under the loose edge of the tape and press the tape. The plastic should completely cover walls and baseboards. To mask woodwork, apply masking or painter's tape along the side edge of window and door trim. Press the edge abutting the wall. If you are painting windows, place tape along the glass edges, leaving a hairline strip of exposed glass. Remove tape after paint dries.

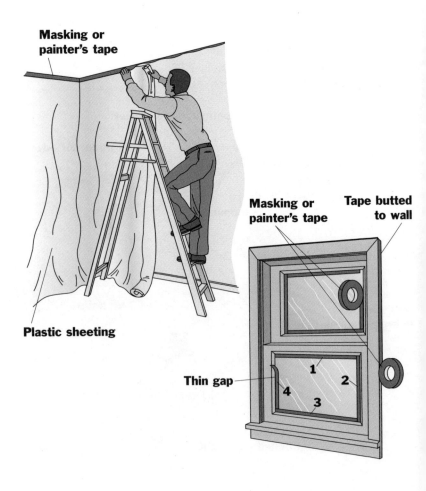

Masking or painter's tape

Plastic sheeting

Masking or painter's tape

Tape butted to wall

Thin gap

1 2 3 4

Clean, prime, and seal

Clean all walls and ceilings with a vacuum cleaner or dust mop. Then wash the surfaces with a household cleaner. Rinse well. Use a solution of chlorine bleach and water to remove mold and mildew, and a degreasing agent to clean grease spots. Apply primer or sealer as directed.

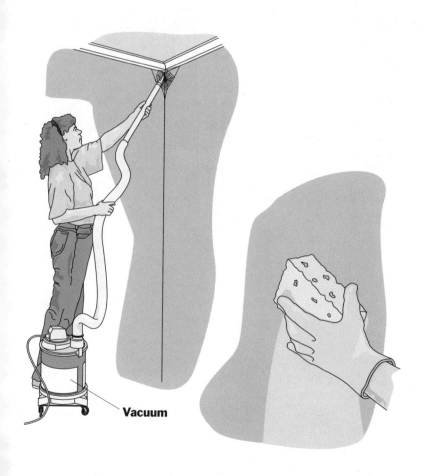

Vacuum

Prepare the paint

Newly purchased paint should be stirred lightly with a clean mixing paddle. The color in custom-mixed cans can vary slightly. To avoid problems, pour all paint for the job into a 5-gallon bucket. Mix thoroughly, then pour the paint back into the cans. Seal the lids on all but the can used immediately. To remove lumps from paint, pour it through a paint strainer into a pail. Discard the lumps. If necessary, thin paint with water or paint thinner.

TIP: Drive small nail holes into the grooves in the paint can rims. This allows the paint to drain back into the can.

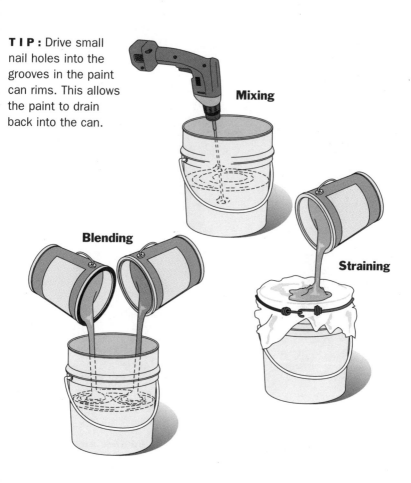

Mixing

Blending

Straining

2

Brush, roller techniques

Hold the brush lightly, with thumb and fingers around the ferrule, not the handle. Dip the bristles only a third of the way into the paint, then lift straight up and slap (don't drag!) lightly against the inside of the can. Holding the brush at a 45-degree angle, apply paint in a long, even stroke, slightly overlapping the edge of the previous stroke. Use long, even strokes to spread the paint from painted to unpainted sections. Feather the ends of the stroke by lifting the brush while still moving through the stroke.

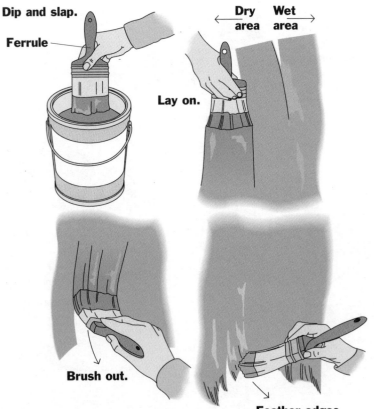

Dip and slap.

Ferrule

Lay on.

← **Dry area** **Wet area** →

Brush out.

Feather edges.

TIP: Always try to face toward the light as you paint. This allows you to see spots that you missed or painted too thinly.

To roll, first rinse the roller with water (latex paint) or mineral spirits (alkyd paint). Fill the tray with paint, dip in the roller, and roll it up the tray to distribute the paint. Work in 6-foot or smaller sections, moving the roller in a series of overlapping **M**s. When you reach the bottom of the last leg of the **M**, work backward, slightly overlapping the previous strokes. Reload the roller as needed. When the section is filled with paint, smooth the paint with light, overlapping, vertical strokes.

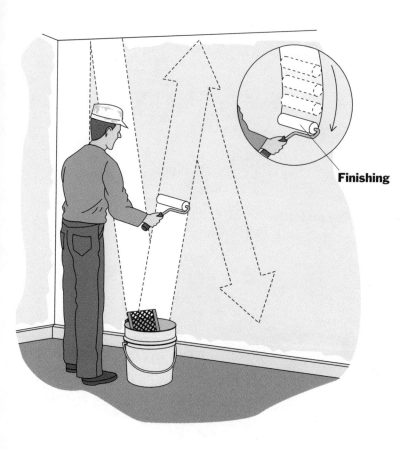

Finishing

3 Ceilings

Paint the ceiling before the walls. Work in 3- to 4-foot sections, cutting in with the trim brush, then rolling the same area. Always maintain a wet edge for the next section. Using a trim brush, first apply a 4-inch strip of paint around the edges and any obstructions, such as light fixtures. When one section has been cut in, use the roller to fill it in with paint. Use the M pattern, blending the paint into the brush strokes. Lift the roller before completing the last stroke.

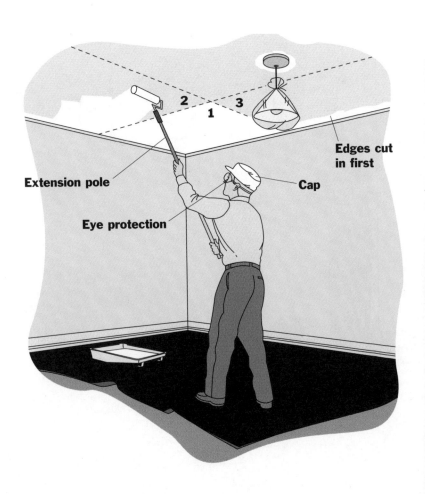

Edges cut in first

Extension pole

Cap

Eye protection

4 Walls

Paint the walls when the ceiling is dry to the touch. Work in sections so you can maintain a wet edge. Plan to finish a full wall before stopping. Cut in a 4-inch strip of paint at the ceiling line, flexing the brush to create a straight, slightly feathered line. Then cut in the corner, along the baseboards, and around any openings or obstructions in that section. When the section has been cut in, immediately roll the wall in Ms, blending into the wet edges.

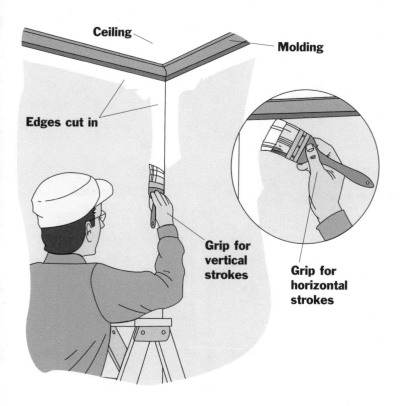

Ceiling

Molding

Edges cut in

Grip for vertical strokes

Grip for horizontal strokes

Windows and doors

Start windows early so that the paint will be dry enough to close them at night. Remove hardware, and open windows. Paint the wood nearest the glass first, working out toward the jambs (but paint the jambs later). Use an angular sash brush, and paint horizontal parts with horizontal strokes, vertical parts with vertical strokes, from top to bottom. Paint a double-hung window in the sequence shown, first reversing the positions of the upper and lower sashes. Don't paint the sash tracks. While drying, move sashes to prevent sticking.

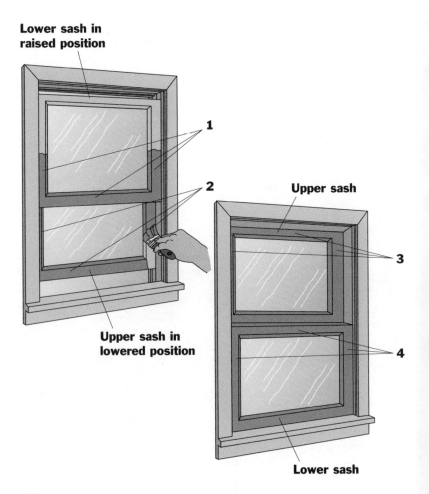

Lower sash in raised position

Upper sash in lowered position

Upper sash

Lower sash

For doors, remove all hardware and, if possible, remove the door and lay it across sawhorses. Paint so that the latch and hinge sides match the rooms they face when the door is open. Paint in sections as dictated by the style of door, as shown. Paint from wet into dry areas, feathering the final strokes. When using alkyd paint on a flush door, apply it with a roller, starting at the center and working out. Use a trim brush to spread and smooth the paint.

Paint out from corners.

Painting Sequence

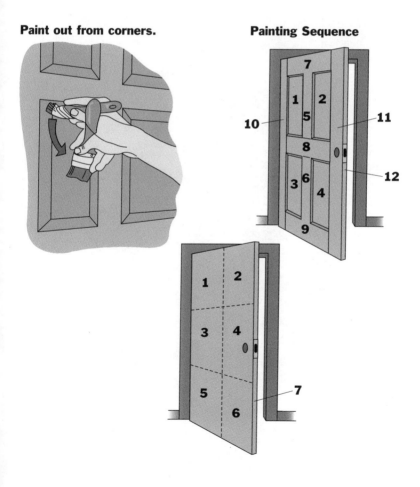

6 Trim, moldings, baseboards

Paint horizontal surfaces with lateral strokes, vertical surfaces from top down. Use a trim brush along the edges nearest the wall. Protect the wall with masking or painter's tape. For windows, open the window slightly, then paint the jamb and stops. Next paint the face trim, from top to bottom. For door trim, first paint the jamb and the edge of the stop facing the door. If the door will be the same color on both sides, paint the entire jamb. Then paint the casing.

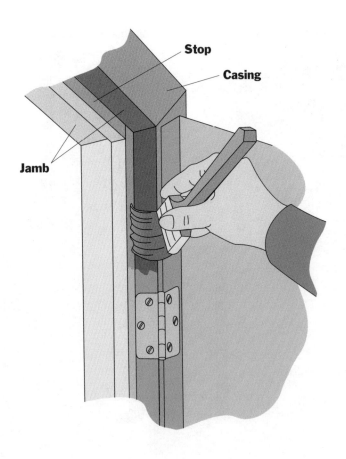

If you have crown, picture, or other moldings to paint, work from the top down. Use the brush that best matches the width of the molding. Paint the top edge first, then the bottom edge. Use a paint shield to pull carpet away from baseboards. Finally, fill in between the edges, finishing with light strokes.

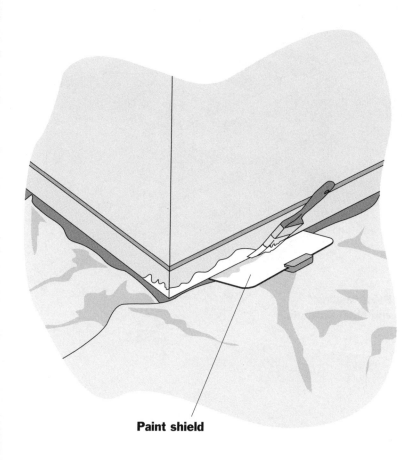

Paint shield

Cabinets and shutters

7

Remove all cabinet hardware, drawers, adjustable shelves, and, if possible, doors. Set them aside. Paint all vertical surfaces from the top down; all horizontal surfaces with lateral strokes. Work in sections, following the sequence shown below. Next paint any sections that were removed. Stand drawers on their backs for painting. Do not paint the drawer openings inside the cabinet.

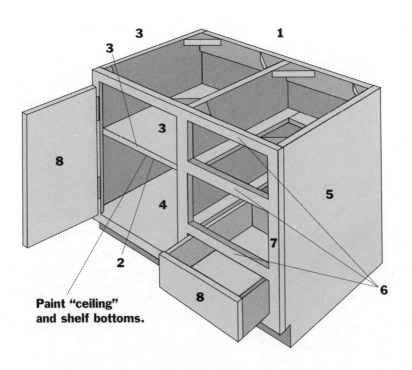

Paint "ceiling" and shelf bottoms.

Remove all hardware and rest shutters on woodblocks. Paint paneled shutters the same as paneled doors (see page 33), except paint both sides and all edges. The easiest way to paint louvered shutters is with a handheld sprayer or aerosol paint. If you use a trim brush, follow this order: (1) With the louvers wide open, paint the inside edges of the frame; (2) paint the top halves of the louvers; (3) turn the shutter and finish louvers and adjusting rod; (4) paint the frame, one side at a time, and outer edges.

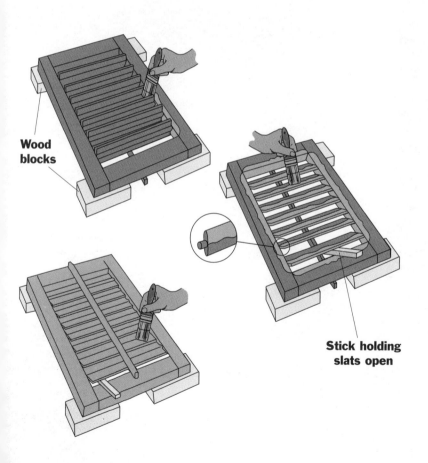

Wood blocks

Stick holding slats open

Decorative Techniques

1 Pattern and texture

Texture paints come premixed or as powdered additives. They are particularly useful for hiding flaws or unevenness in walls. A textured finish also breaks up the monotony of smooth surfaces. Prepare the paint as directed, then practice your technique on scrap pieces of wallboard, wood, or cardboard. Apply the paint with a long-nap roller to create a stippled effect. Alternatively, roll on the paint in sections, then create textures and patterns by dabbing, dragging, or swirling with a sponge, whisk broom, dry paintbrush, or rag.

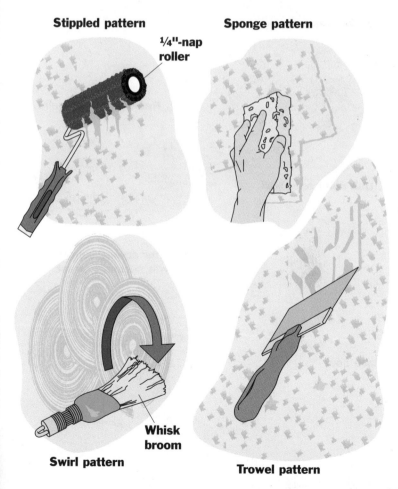

Stippled pattern

¼"-nap roller

Sponge pattern

Swirl pattern

Whisk broom

Trowel pattern

2

Sponge

Sponging involves applying two or more topcoats over the base coat, then finishing with a wash or glaze. Natural sponges create the most interesting effects. Apply the base coat. When it has dried, put on latex gloves and dampen the sponge. Dip the sponge into the paint, then dab it on a piece of cardboard to remove excess paint. Gently tap the sponge on the wall in a random pattern. Let each topcoat dry before sponging the next layer. Dilute the base color and dab it lightly over the wall.

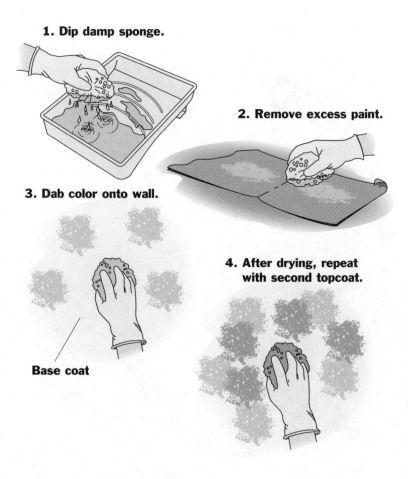

1. Dip damp sponge.

2. Remove excess paint.

3. Dab color onto wall.

4. After drying, repeat with second topcoat.

Base coat

Rag roll

Rag rolling is similar to sponging. Use contrasting colors for bold effects, similar colors for muted effects. Use clean, lint-free rags (cotton diapers or cheesecloth cut into 18-inch squares). When the base coat dries, dip the rag in paint (wear gloves), wring it out slightly, and twist into a roll. Starting in a corner, slowly roll the rag from the top, allowing plenty of base color to show through the first topcoat. Change rags frequently. When dry, apply a second topcoat, overlapping the first. Finish with diluted base paint.

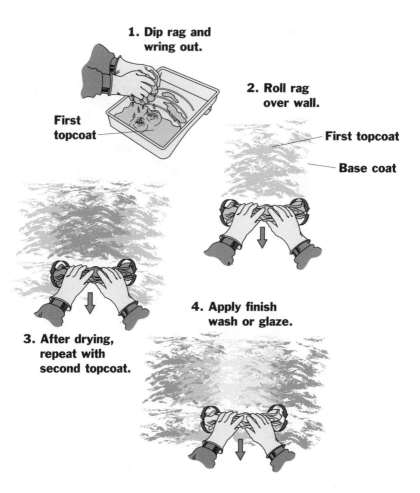

1. Dip rag and wring out.

First topcoat

2. Roll rag over wall.

First topcoat

Base coat

3. After drying, repeat with second topcoat.

4. Apply finish wash or glaze.

Color wash

Color washing creates walls with a soft, aged appearance. The topcoats are thinned latex or alkyd paint. The amount of thinning is a personal choice, but 9 parts water or mineral spirits to 1 part paint is typical. Apply the base coat. When dry, apply the first topcoat with a flat brush. Avoid an even look: Move the brush randomly, varying the size, shape, and direction of strokes, allowing plenty of background to show through. Brush out any hard edges. When dry, apply one or more additional topcoats, overlapping previous strokes.

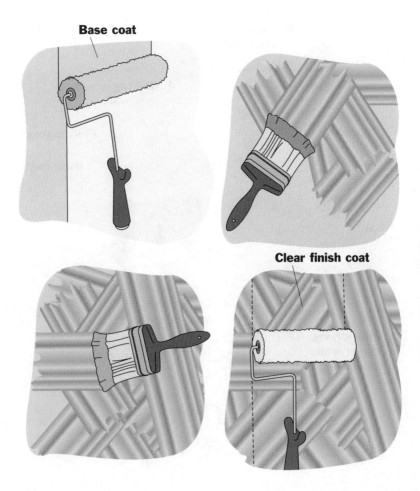

Base coat

Clear finish coat

5

Drag and comb

Dragging involves applying a glaze coat of thinned alkyd paint (latex dries too fast), then removing some of it before it dries. It requires a steady hand, practice, and a partner. Apply a base coat. When dry, apply a thin strip of glaze with a roller. Your partner should immediately pull the dragging tool from the ceiling to the baseboard. Use a dry brush to drag straight lines, or cut notches in a rubber squeegee and drag a curved pattern. Clean the dragging tool after each use. Overlap roller strokes.

Strips of glaze removed by squeegee or brush

Base coat **Glaze coat**

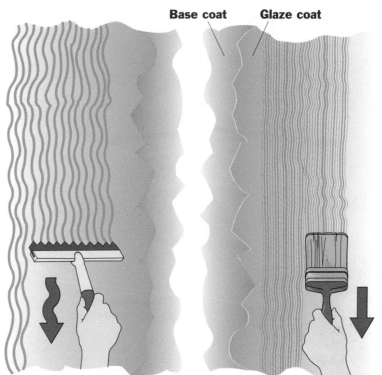

Stencil

You can paint stencils on any clean, dry surface. Buy stencils at arts-and-crafts stores, or make your own. Use latex paints or artist's acrylics, applied with flat stencil brushes. Each color requires a separate stencil. Measure and mark the stencil locations on the wall. Use masking tape to anchor the stencil in position. Dip the stencil brush in paint, dabbing the excess on cardboard. Paint over the cutout, working from edges to the center. Carefully lift and reposition the stencil, cleaning it as necessary.

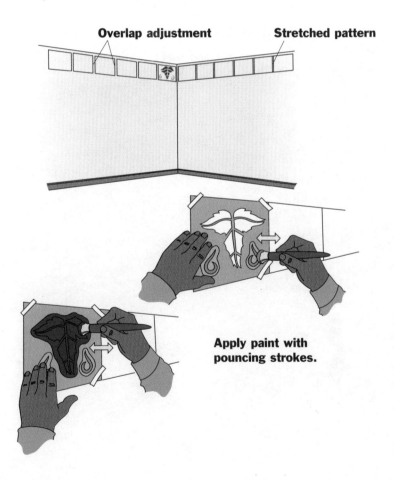

Overlap adjustment   **Stretched pattern**

Apply paint with pouncing strokes.

To make your own stencil design, look for patterns or ideas
in decorating magazines or stencil pattern books, or draw
your own. Make one stencil for each color. If you copy a
design, use carbon paper to trace it directly onto acetate or
stencil paper, or copy the design freehand using graph
paper to improve accuracy. Make all the bridges (partitions
between cutout areas in the stencil) at least ¼ inch. Use a
utility knife to carefully make the cutouts. Mark each stencil
so you can align the layers during painting.

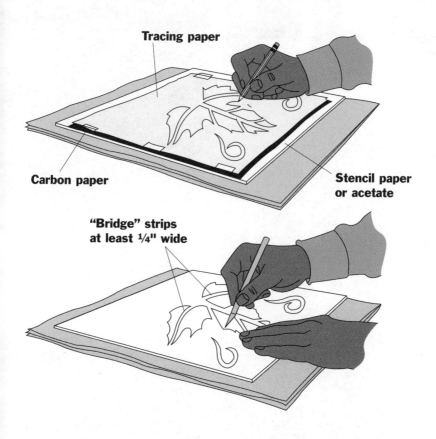

Tracing paper

Carbon paper

**Stencil paper
or acetate**

**"Bridge" strips
at least ¼" wide**

Painting Exteriors

Choose a color scheme

Find inspiration in magazines and by looking at other houses, especially houses similar to yours. Consider the effects of the roof (color and pitch), trees, plants, garages, and neighboring structures. Browse paint stores for swatches with colors and combinations that interest you. Take them home, where you can study them against your own house under natural light. Experiment with analogous and complementary combinations. Choose paint to complement unpainted brick or stone siding.

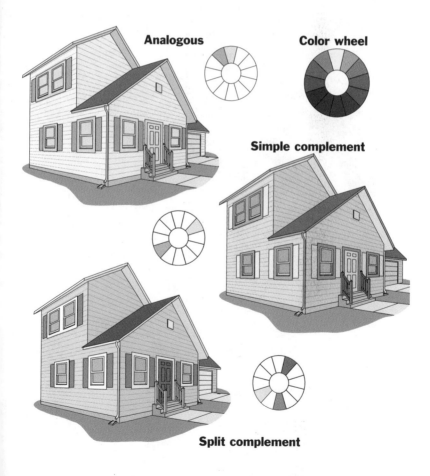

Analogous

Color wheel

Simple complement

Split complement

2 Prepare wood surfaces

Scrape all loose paint from siding and trim, working downward from the top of the house. Use molding scrapers for hard-to-reach spots. Scrape with the grain of the wood. Wear a hat, dust mask, goggles, and gloves. Use a power sander to smooth the wood and remove excess paint. When scraping or sanding, take care not to gouge the wood. If you want to completely remove paint from trim or doors, use a heat gun or chemical stripper as directed by the manufacturer.

Drop cloth

3

Prepare metal surfaces

Use a rigid scraper to remove loose paint and rust, then go over the surface with a wire brush (or wire-brush attachment on an electric drill). Apply a metal primer immediately to prevent rust from reappearing. New iron or steel should be cleaned with a solvent before priming. Galvanized metal should be treated with metal etch (as directed by the manufacturer) or primed with an appropriate primer. Do not sand or scrape galvanized metal unless the zinc coating has worn away and rust is present.

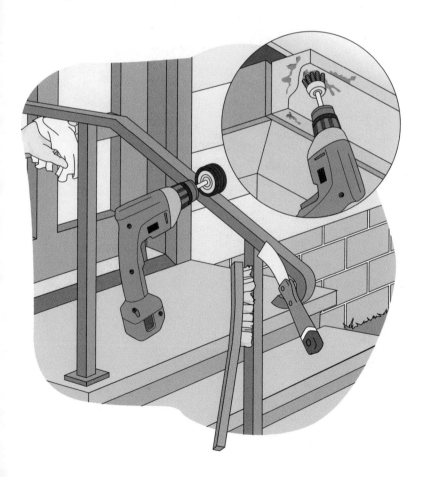

4 Prepare masonry

Fill holes in brick and concrete block with a block filler. Remove and replace crumbling mortar. Repair stucco with ready-mixed stucco patch. Use a dry, stiff-bristled brush to remove all loose debris and surface stains. Primers are available for creating a smooth finish over concrete block or other rough and porous masonry surfaces. Normal alkyd primers usually work well on masonry.

Fill holes with block filler.

5

Clean surfaces

Paint will last much longer when applied to a surface free of dirt, grease, and mildew. Starting at the top, scrub exterior surfaces with a strong detergent, such as a trisodium phosphate (TSP) substitute. Use a large brush or rent a power washer. Because it operates under such high pressure, a power washer can minimize the need for scraping. Rinse with a garden hose. Clean mildew with a solution of water and chlorine bleach; let dry, but don't rinse. Let the house dry for a couple of days before painting.

Power washer

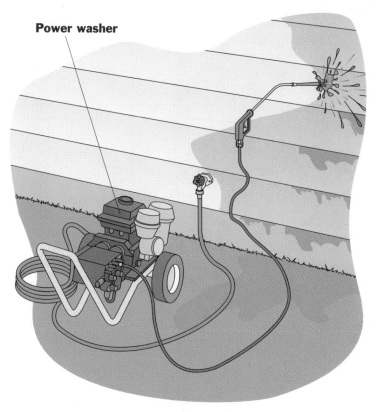

TIP: A power washer is efficient, but it is no toy. Read the instructions carefully and use extra caution when working from a ladder.

 Set up painting site

Standard canvas drop cloths are best because they absorb paint, are rugged enough to walk on, and are heavy enough to stay in place. Plastic tarps are a viable substitute, but should be tied down. Old bedsheets are ideal for covering delicate plants. Cover walkways, patios, and decks. When brushing or rolling, protect surfaces at least 6 feet from the wall. When spraying, cover an even wider area and mask windows and other surfaces. Keep plants away from the house by trimming or tying them back.

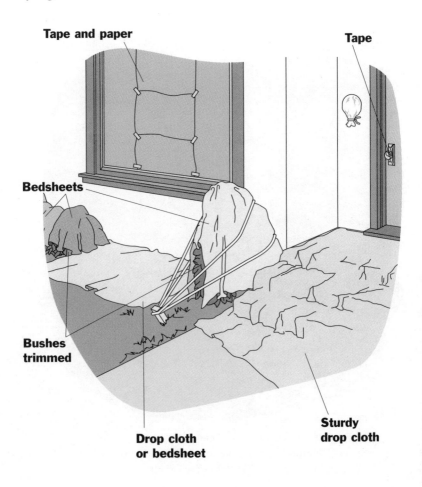

Tape and paper

Tape

Bedsheets

Bushes trimmed

Drop cloth or bedsheet

Sturdy drop cloth

Make sure all ladders are in good condition and are resting on level, solid ground. Don't exceed the load-bearing capacity of a ladder. Position extension ladders at a safe angle. Set up and inspect scaffolding carefully. Ladder jacks allow you to attach a plank between two extension ladders, but should be used only with heavy-duty ladders. Affordable accessories hold ladders away from windows, gutters, and corners. Don't stand on the top of a stepladder or lean out over the sides of an extension ladder.

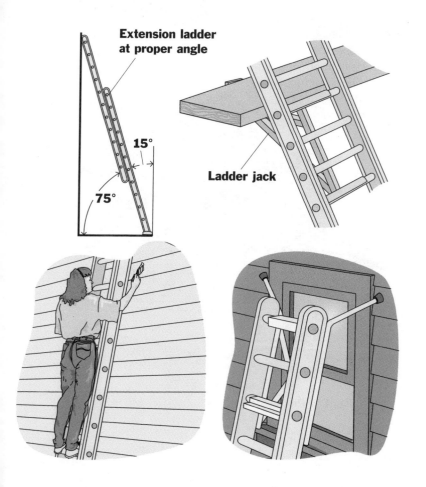

Extension ladder at proper angle

15°

75°

Ladder jack

Apply paint

Professional painters "paint in the shade" or "follow the sun." Avoid painting in direct sunlight. Instead, try to paint a wall after the sun has passed and the side has begun to cool. Work from the top down. Try to reach a visual breakpoint before stopping. Allow one color to dry completely before applying an adjacent color. Paint soffits and roof trim first (if they will be different colors), and leave surfaces to be stained until after the painting is done. The house should be dry, and the weather forecast favorable.

TIP: When painting siding that contains asbestos, do not sand or otherwise cut or abrade the surface. Check with a qualified professional regarding repairs or removal.

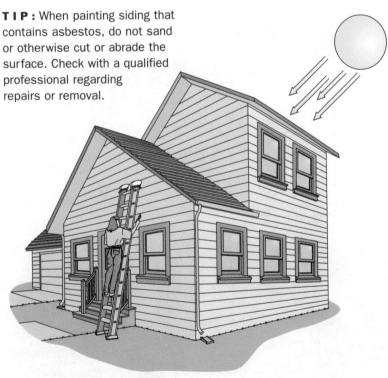

Paint in the shade.

See pages 27 to 37 for advice on mixing paint, using brushes and rollers, and cleaning up. On wide-board siding, lay on paint with a brush or roller, then use a brush or beveled roller to paint the edges. Brush out the paint with horizontal strokes. Work in sections, feathering (gradually placing and lifting the brush or roller) and maintaining a wet edge. Narrow clapboard or shingle siding should be brushed or sprayed. Sprayers vary, so follow manufacturer's instructions carefully. Avoid spraying on windy days, and wear a spray sock and respirator.

1. Lay on paint with a roller.

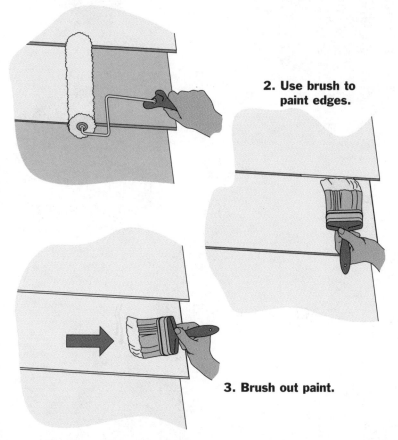

2. Use brush to paint edges.

3. Brush out paint.

1

Peeling and blistering

When a paint job fails prematurely, it's wise to find and fix the cause before trying to cover it up. When chunks of paint begin separating from the surface, or small blisters appear, the cause may be poor surface preparation (too dirty or greasy). Also, moisture may be trying to escape from inside the house, or rainwater is getting behind the paint. If the problem affects a large area, it could indicate a serious moisture problem in the house or that the wrong type of paint was used.

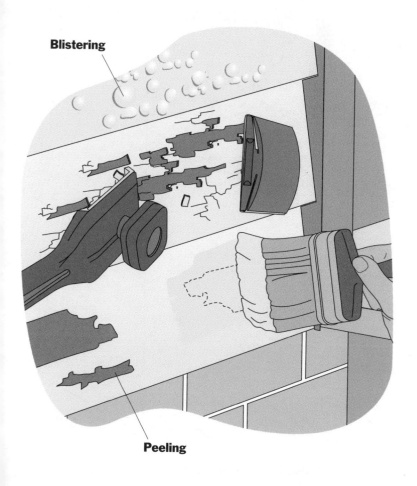

Blistering

Peeling

2 Loose window putty

Replace loose or cracked putty (glazing compound) around window glass before painting. Remove the old putty with a putty knife or glazier's chisel. Form new putty into a rope and push it in place. Use a putty knife to smooth, and remove the excess. If completely reglazing the window, remove glazing points and glass, and lightly sand the frame. Seal the exposed wood. When dry, spread a thin layer of putty on the frame to seal the edges of the window. Press the glass in place, push in new glazing points, and apply putty.

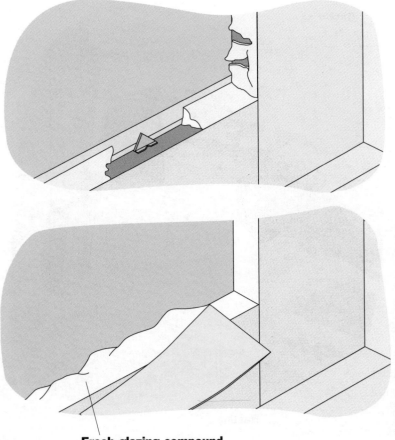

Fresh glazing compound

3 Alligatoring

When cracks that resemble an alligator's hide appear in paint, the cause can be that the paint was applied under direct sunlight (causing it to dry too quickly), or that the surface (or the first coat) wasn't allowed to dry thoroughly before paint was applied. Alligatoring can also occur when paint has been applied too thickly. If the problem is in only a small area, it could be due to poor surface preparation. Scrape completely before repainting.

4 Chalking

No paint job will last forever. When a painted surface starts producing a layer that resembles chalk dust, most often it is merely showing the signs of natural aging. As the binders in the paint begin breaking down, they leave behind a film of pigment that is evident when you run your hand over it. Rain, or a good washing with a hose, should remove the chalky surface to reveal a clean layer of paint. Chalk should always be washed off before repainting.

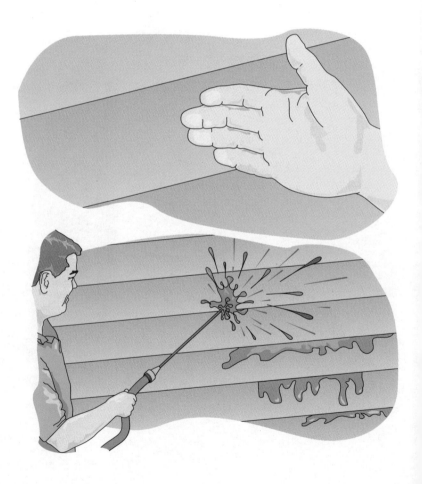

Bleeding

Some types of softwood (such as pine) contain rosin that will "bleed" through paint, especially around knots. Before painting, coat the wood with a stain-killing primer/sealer or shellac. If rust bleeds through a painted metal surface (including nail heads), wash or scrape off the stains, then apply a metal primer before repainting. Rusting nails and screws should be replaced with hot-dipped galvanized fasteners.

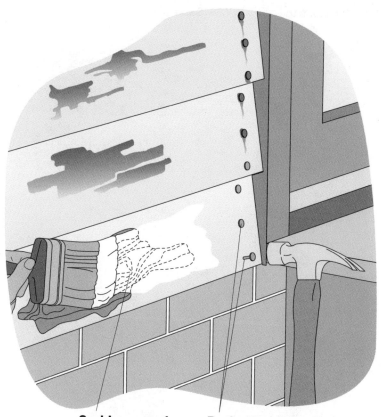

Seal bare wood with stain-killing primer/sealer.

Replace rusted nails with hot-dipped galvanized nails.

6 Touch up

Keep extra paint on hand for the inevitable touch-ups. Transfer small amounts of paint into quart paint cans or tightly sealed glass jars. Label the containers. Before touching up, prepare the surface as you did for the original paint job. Scrape away all loose paint, then sand the face and edges to create a smooth surface. Remove all dirt and grease. When dry, apply paint with a small brush. Build up thin layers of paint to match the surrounding surface.

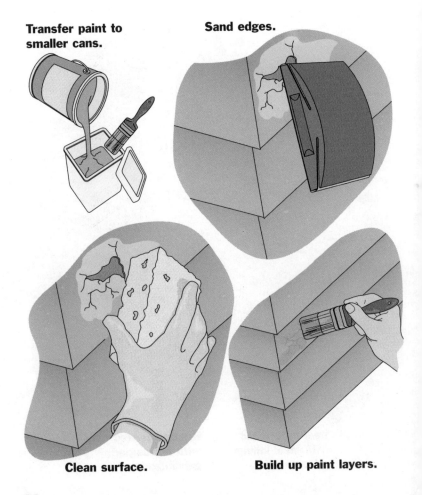

Transfer paint to smaller cans.

Sand edges.

Clean surface.

Build up paint layers.